Happy Birthday
Love,
Ken And Becky

Goin' Down the River

Fish Camps of the Sea Islands

Janet H. Garrity

Foreword by Gibbes McDowell

Lydia Inglett Ltd. Publishing
MMXII

Goin' Down the River
Fish Camps of the Sea Islands

Foreword by
Gibbes McDowell

Janet H. Garrity

Goin' Down the River
Fish Camps of the Sea Islands

by Janet H. Garrity

Copyright © 2012
ISBN: 978-1-938417-01-6

All rights reserved, no portion of this book may be reproduced, stored in a retrieval system, or transmitted in any form, or by any means – mechanical, electronic, photocopying, recording or otherwise – without prior written permission from the publisher and author, except as provided by United States of America copyright law. Printed in China.

Lydia Inglett Ltd. Publishing
301 Central Avenue #181
Hilton Head Island, SC 29926
www.lydiainglett.com
www.starbooks.biz

www.garrity.com

In Memory of Alex Spencer

I joyfully dedicate this book to my friend Alex Spencer, who left our world on April 15, 2011. If Alex had not come into my life, this book would not be sitting in front of you. The concept of documenting the Sea Islands' fish camps came through Alex. He first told me about this project in 2010, and when I asked whether I could assist, he said "I don't want you to assist, I want you to partner with me." So the journey began, each of us seeing through our lens a different angle, a different light, a unique perspective, but we were sharing the same energy and loving life.

After a couple of shoots, the weather turned cold, so we took a break for a few months. Sadly, Alex never got back out on the water. For the prior three years, he had been in a fight for his life against colon cancer and the effects of the disease. At one point, as his body failed him, I asked Alex whether he would like me to finish what we had started together, and his response was, "I'd be honored." So in honor of Alex, I present you with *Goin' Down the River, Fish Camps of the Sea Islands*. I hope I have made you proud, Alex.

Preface

This book is a collection of old and current photographs of fish camps scattered about the Sea Islands. The current photographs of the camps were taken by me. The older photos came to me via gracious individuals who searched their family albums and personal files. These kind people are given credit later in the book. As requested, recognition has been given to photographers of several of the older photos.

All but one of the fish camps that I photographed are privately owned properties. The single exception is the abandoned camp situated on an island owned by the state of South Carolina. My promise to the property owners was, and continues to be, that the camps would not be individually profiled and their locations would not be disclosed. These camps are not open to the public.

There are assorted stories and quotes included in the book that were either told to me or written for the book. Those that were written for the book include credit to the author, unless requested otherwise. When the story came from a personal interview, I either paraphrased or quoted the person and referenced my source. The writings that do not give credit to an author or source are my writings. I have spent many, many hours gathering information for this book, with the goal that readers find that I have represented the facts accurately. I trust that will be the case, but if there are errors in the facts, I take full responsibility.

- Janet Garrity

Foreword

By Gibbes McDowell

It's 6:00 pm on a cool October Friday afternoon in the Lowcountry. The setting sun is about to surrender the day with its final pink and orange painting of the western skyline. A fall moon rising in the east and pushing a nine-foot tide has the marsh hens cackling as I back my boat down the ramp. Deep draughts of cool salty air quicken my anticipation of the weekend to come.

The outboard motor fires on the first pull and all my problems are left suspended on "the hill" (the boat ramp) behind me. The world will just have to wait until I get back. I'm goin' down the river to a fish camp to meet lifelong friends for a weekend of fishing, cooking, and storytelling around the campfire. It's a place where we all have nicknames. The stories fly fast, getting better and better with the retelling.

"Do you remember that guy who did two back flips off the dock into the pluff mud and never spilled his beer?"

"Or how 'bout the old timer who watered down the oyster gravy with naphtha instead of water? Damn near killed us all."

These are the best days of our lives. Who says you can never go home again?

This day Trenchards Inlet is rough. I can clearly hear my father's voice tutoring me as a youngster learning how to handle a boat.

"In rough water you have to feather the throttle to keep the boat at just the right speed so you don't submarine the bow or take water over the stern. Make your decisions fast and don't hesitate. Trenchards can kill you."

The 30-minute ride is comfortably cold, reminding me of many such trips with my Dad and the fish camps we shared. Forty years later, his spirit is still with me at every campfire or oyster roast. Whether fishing the surf for redfish, or sneaking up on an island duck pond, his teachings have stood me well. My father's experiences pass through my own, like a fine seasoning, on to my son, who, with his friends, is building his own fish camp resume.

Coming around the last bend in the creek I can smell it first; the siren smell of an oak fire and then barbecue on the grill. Distant figures dance in the beckoning glow. When my boat slides up against the dock, a friend with a ceremonial Budweiser steps out of the darkness to welcome me to the camp. The warmth of the open fire brings me into my circle of friends. I have made it. I am on hallowed ground. I'm "down the river."

The Story of Fish Camps

Scattered around the South Carolina Sea Islands are camps that have become very special places to generations of families and friends in the Lowcountry. These camps are referred to as fish camps. Full of character and fairly remote, the camps are accessible only by water and, therefore, exclusive (as well as reclusive, if need be). These camps have been witness to so many life experiences and lessons that you can almost hear the memories whispering to you as you step from the boat to the dock.

"Goin' down the river" is what one does to get to the camp, but the phrase means so much more than "I'm putting the boat in the water and going to the camp." The phrase is sort of a code to those who know the fish camp experience. On the simplest level, it means "We're going to have some fun." On a more complex level, "goin' down the river" means a retreat for the mind, body and soul. It's about getting away.

Getting away to the Sea Islands has been going on for more than 250 years. Camping on the outer islands can be traced back to Native Americans who moved to the islands in the summer months to hunt and fish. For modern man, the use of the islands for recreation began in the 1730's, according to Dr. Lawrence Rowland, historian and professor emeritus at the University of South Carolina Beaufort and an author of "The History of Beaufort County, South Carolina, Volume I 1514-1861." During the plantation era, white men navigated row boats to the uninhabited islands, taking with them camping tents, slaves, and dogs, to fish the waters and to hunt for deer, wild boar, and water fowl. By the 1750's, the activity was fairly sophisticated. Hunting parties would make camp and stay for a week, returning to their plantations with boat loads of venison or whatever game had been hunted on that week's expedition.[1]

In the late 18th century, wealthy planters began to resort to the Sea Islands for the beaches and the cooler temperatures. Whereas the hunting and fishing camps were primarily male dominated, women took part in the migrations to the

Marooning in the 1890's.

beach camps. This activity was referred to as "marooning." Men, women, and children traveled by boat, taking food staples and camping necessities. Men fished and hunted and women cooked the catch of the day. The more popular islands were those most easily reached based on the tides. Bay Point, located on the edge of the Atlantic to the north side of the Port Royal Sound, was an extremely popular destination for marooning because it was only two tides from Beaufort, SC.[2] Edisto Beach, SC was also a favored destination with the planters. Permanent camps were built on both of these beaches by the frequent marooners, who returned many a time during the summer, and, if the camp survived the winter storms, would migrate there again the following summer season. When the Civil War began in 1860, marooning was discontinued as Union forces took over the islands, including Bay Point in 1861, as defensive positions. After the War, marooning on the Sea Islands, or fish camping, as it is known today, began again, but it was no longer a planter's activity, as the plantation era ended when the Civil War began.[3]

More and more people started marooning at the turn of the 20th century as steamboats and private yachts made regular trips to the outer island beaches. Dr. Rowland states, "Between 1900 and 1905, crowds of people went to the beach for the day and returned in time for the baseball game. It had become a resort activity. The 'real marooners,' those who loved camping in the wild, had to find less accessible places to go."

Fathers, sons and grandsons found remote spits of land down the river where they could get away from everyday life. These hunting and fishing trips to the Sea Islands became a generational tradition for many, with fathers and grandfathers passing on to their young men the art of handling a boat, a gun and a fishing rod, and how to camp and survive the journey. It could take a day or more to reach an island, with an overnight in a bateau not uncommon. The boat was loaded with the necessities: fishing rods, lard, and flour, a block of ice wrapped in burlap, and perhaps a shotgun or a rifle for hunting.

The "Owanee," a yacht owned by Fredrick W. Scheper, made trips to Bay Point in the 1920's. The Pilot of the Owanee was a Mr. Hoffman.

Camps often started as tent sites. When a permanent fish camp was built, it was a slow process. Tin, lumber, nails, tools, and amenities, such as a woodstove, were taken to the island the only way they could get there, by boat, one boatload at a time. The builders of the camps were not necessarily the owners of the islands. Often land owners lived a good distance away and rarely used the property themselves, so camps were built with a simple lease or a handshake agreement with the island's owner. Agreements were relaxed. Friends used friends' islands for hunting and fishing, and camps were used pretty freely as well, as long as everyone was respectful of the other guy's camp and property. Everyone worked on the honor system. Henry C. Chambers, a lifelong resident of Beaufort, SC, and past fish camp owner, said "You didn't have to worry about leaving anything at the camp. No one was going to take it." [4]

Today, those who have had the experience of "going to the camp" recall times in their youth when days were filled with water, sun, fishing, hunting, tall tales, sunburn, practical jokes, sand, mosquitoes, and eating and sleeping. Today there are more bridges and roads, and faster boats, so goin' down the river doesn't take as long as it used to, but perhaps this is not entirely a good thing because getting there was part of the experience. It was common for boys to be turned loose to set off in a bateau to camp on an island for a few days. Their fathers and grandfathers taught them how to watch out for rattlesnakes, how to walk in the pluff mud, and how to catch their supper and cook it over a fire. The young men knew where to go to fish and where to go to hunt

Fishing and camping on Fripp Island, August 1926.

duck, deer or wild boar. They knew how to bait a crab trap and how to use a cast net or a seine net to catch their breakfast. These young men are today's fathers and mentors who are now taking their turn at passing on what it means to go down the river, keeping a sweet tradition alive for another generation.

For a very long time, the Sea Islands were generally open for anyone to use. But as the pressure of development began, and the value of land increased, it changed the relaxed atmosphere because the land started to close up. Some knew things were going to change. A hunter who frequently camped on St. Phillips Island is quoted as saying, "I remember camping out there when the lights came on at Fripp [Island]. That was the beginning of the end." Fripp's development began in the 1960's.[5]

In the 1990's the state of South Carolina claimed ownership of the Sea Islands that were not privately owned. (The state's goal was, and is, to protect the ecosystem on and around the Sea Islands for the benefit of all the people of South Carolina.) Additionally, some privately owned islands have been donated to the state. If fish camps were present under a lease agreement when the state took possession, it became the state's decision whether to renew those leases when they expired. Some were not renewed. Subsequently, camps had to be abandoned, and most were later torn down by the state. The fish camps now are all privately owned or leased. "The days of just going out and using someone's property or because you do the owner favors is gone. It's not the way camping started, but it's a necessity now to own the land or have a solid lease," Dr. Rowland explained. As usually is the unfortunate case, government regulations make what may have been once simple, a complex situation. It's a fine balancing act between the rights of all involved.

Maybe the modern day fish camp is about survival. Maybe it's about the life that vibrates around the Sea Islands. The salt water, the marshes, the sounds, the smells are teaming with energy for all the senses. There is a richness about fish camps that comes not from the structures themselves, but from the synergy of man and nature living together on these spits of land, both being what they are supposed to be while finding a compatibility, a connection, that one doesn't feel "in town." At camp, city lights are replaced with stars. The noise of the television is replaced by the night sounds of the marsh. And the glow of the computer screen is replaced by the glow of a campfire. What is given up to be at the camp is given back with life experiences, experiences that matter.

1. Information gathered during interview with Dr. Lawrence Rowland.

2. The trip would take two outgoing tides to get there. The party would row with the outgoing tide as far as possible then pull their boat up on a nearby hammock to wait out the incoming tide change. The travelers might rest, eat, and swim, and sometimes spend the night, while they waited. When the tide turned out to sea once again, the boat would be launched and they would continue on their way, reaching Bay Point before the next tide change.

3. Information gathered during interview with Dr. Rowland.

4. Information gathered during interview with Henry C. Chambers.

5. Information gathered during interview with Dr. Rowland.

Getting Your Stuff There

It's no easy feat to transport to an island what is needed to build and equip a camp. Everything has to be brought in by boat: lumber, water tanks, wood stoves, refrigerators, generators, mattresses, sinks, furniture, and all "the stuff" that puts that personal touch on the camp. Once the boat arrives at the camp's dock, which also was brought in piece by piece, the cargo has to be unloaded and everything moved to the desired location. In some cases, the move can be lengthy. The answer is brute strength or wheels. (When was the last time you carried a refrigerator?)

Above: A barge and escort boat headed to a camp.
Right: This four-wheeler and boat trailer live on the island, subject to the salt air and sandy winds, for the purpose of transporting to the camp what is brought in by boat. In the background, a pontoon boat anchored in the inlet brought a family and supplies to their camp for a maroon.

"And as we went, we'd take a 2 x 4 or some planking, or some tin, and eventually build the camp, that we'd go back to time and time again, piece by piece."

- Henry Chambers

Sandy Peabody and his son, Clark Rowland Peabody, age three, take a father-and-son hike at low tide while at their family's fish camp in 2008.

Machete Flats

By Gibbes McDowell

Glen Kilgore and I were spending a weekend at Johnson Creek Camp re-thatching the palmetto roofed cabana on our dock. This takes two days of hard work, three boat loads of palmetto fronds, and a cooler full of Budweiser. We scoured every marsh hammock in sight for the palmettos we needed, cutting them with machete and bush ax. At the end of a long day's work and with the bottom of the beer cooler in sight, we motored our boat up to the end of a long skinny island in Harbor River. The island had no name we were aware of, but it did have a nice stand of palmettos. The tide was high. An orange sunset cast a golden glow across the marsh. We stopped to enjoy the moment. Life was good.

Suddenly, a splash near the boat drew our attention to a host of waving hands. Waving hands? How many beers have you had? Those are tailing bass! A quick look around the boat found not a single fishing rod, or even a cast net. They had been left at the dock to make room for palmettos. Glen was not to be denied. He grabbed his machete and eased over the side into shin deep water. His Budweiser stealth was less than cat like. Wiser to let the fish come to him. Soon a large spot tail came cruising towards Glen. With machete raised at the ready, he launched a furious assault on the unsuspecting fish. Slashing the water to a froth produced howls of laughter from me and one long gone bass.

Borrowing a phrase from the late newsman, Paul Harvey, I close this piece in saying, "and now for the rest of the story." Glen and I later came to own this island and several others around it. When we eventually sold them to become part of Hunting Island State Park we had to place names on the islands. This one became known as Machete Flats.

Male Sanctuaries

Fish camps tend to be male sanctuaries. That is not to say there aren't many weekends at the camp with the family, nor is it to imply that women aren't allowed. What it does say is that men built the camps to be simple and low on luxuries (in most cases, this is still true). The camps have hand-me-down furniture. The sleeping arrangements are bunk beds stacked in bunk houses and the main camp. Frequently, there are no private sleeping arrangements to be made, unless you're willing to pitch a tent. Nowadays, some camps have generators to run air conditioning, but many folks have kept the tradition of keeping their camp's facilities to a minimum. After all, part of the beauty of fish camps is their rustic atmosphere. So let's put it this way, not all women want to "rough it" at fish camp, and not on all occasions are women invited. Enough said about that.

"The first time I went to a fish camp, I asked the camp owner, 'Does a lot of fishing go on at fish camp?'

"He casually replied, 'No, not really. A lot of other things go on, but not much fishing.'"

- Janet Garrity

5 minutes later - Dinner's ready

The boys of summer.

A "meeting" at the Vaigneur's camp, next to the Bay Point camp.

"If there is a heaven on earth, I would call it a fish camp in Trenchards Inlet."

- Lew Gibson

Nature

A **raccoon trail** through the low-tide marsh leads from one hammock to another. During low tide, raccoons feed on the oysters, mussels, and clams in the marsh and look for fresh water around the camps. Camp cisterns, the only source for fresh water at the camps, are made "raccoon-proof" to prevent contamination of the water.

Raccoons will also feast on sea turtle eggs. When the female turtles come ashore at night on the outlying Sea Islands to lay their eggs, the raccoons in the vicinity will sit by the nest and wait while the turtle lays her eggs. Once she is finished and has moved off, the raccoons dig up the nest and devour the eggs. The evidence is seen here that nature will always take her course, and at times it is an unpleasant sight.

"We're in the middle of Nowhere,
but we're on the middle of Everywhere."

- Scott Stowe, *taken from a fish camp journal*

Conch Shells

The **conch shells** that are scattered around today's fish camps, bleached by the elements, may have been washed up on shore by passing storms and incoming tides, or they were left by Native Americans, who inhabited the Sea Islands thousands of years ago. Indians used the Sea Islands as hunting and fishing grounds in the summer months, migrating from the mainland where they wintered. Conch was one of the food supplies natural to the islands. The Indians drilled holes in the back of the shells to remove the conch to cook it. Pyramids of conch shells, all with drilled holes, have been found on the islands under layers of dirt, indicating that the shells may have been there for at least one thousand years. It's believed that the Indians used their own version of fish camps on the Sea Islands as a mode of survival long before modern man began using them for recreational hunting and fishing.[6]

6. Information gathered during interview with Dr. Rowland.

Fresh Water Pond

There is a fresh water pond located deep within one of the Sea Islands, near where several fish camps once existed but are no longer, that is a painter's dream of the Garden of Eden. It is pure beauty to the eyes and the ears. The plants are lush and a vivid green. The bird life abounds – wood storks and heron flock and nest in the trees. Listen and you can hear their calls and the sound of their wings as they take flight from the water's edge when intruded upon. Deer tracks are scattered in the soft mud, as are raccoon prints and other small animal tracks.

Just like the Garden of Eden, under every beautiful surface is the less beautiful. The water breeds millions of mosquitoes. There are so many that it's of no use to swat them off, because I may kill a dozen, but there are hundreds more on my clothes and exposed skin. So I try to ignore them as I "quietly" maneuver through the overgrown jungle surrounding the pond. At each step, I watch for snakes and listen for any sound that resembles the grunt of a gator. Yes, there is a gator hole in the pond. When the jungle gives up and the pond emerges, it's like no other place in the world that I've seen. The full understanding now sinks in … nature is why some folks are drawn to go down the river. It is an awesome, almost otherworldly, convergence with nature. And if I hadn't been worrying about the gators showing up and how many ticks I'd have picked off when I got home, I could have stayed all day.

Marooning on Bay Point

The McLeod and Poulnot families built this camp on Bay Point and took their families here for many years. When the camp was built it sat back in the woods a bit, but by the mid-1990's, when these photos were taken, erosion had taken away a portion of the beach and the salt water had killed the front lines of trees. In later years, the two families sold the island, and it has since gone through various owners, including a Saudi prince.

Camp on Bay Point 1928.

"They built a dock so they could tie up, because [the camp] was right on the ocean on Bay Point, so they would come up through an inlet on the back of the island, and then it was a long trek through the woods. Eventually, they put a tractor on the island so they would haul provisions and whatever when they'd go down there, because they would go and stay, and they would love it."

- Marjorie Fordham Trask; *her grandfather was Claude E. McLeod, speaking about her family goin' down the river to Bay Point*

Top: The "gang" at Bay Point, 1917.

Bottom Left: Aboard the yacht "Zorayda," Hope McLeod watches from the bow as the seine net is mended. At the turn of the century, yachts like this took folks out to the beaches, including Bay Point, to maroon.

Bottom Right: Preparing the seine, May 1961 at Bay Point. L to R: Jimmy Bishop, Butch Wilson, Barney Rhett, Pat Calhoun and George F. Ricker.

"What goes on down the river,
stays down the river."

- Lew Gibson

Missing Silver

We used to live out on a little island in the Burton area. We had to build a causeway to get over to it. It was called Sandy Ridge Island. Right off of Sandy Ridge is a small island and there was no way to get to it except by boat, and [that island] was the camping place for every boy growing up, including my own three sons. It was just a hop, skip and a jump from Sandy Ridge, where we lived. The boys could bog across at low tide, meaning they waded through mud up to their knees.

One day one of my boys came home and said, "Mama, look what we found over on the island."

"What?" I asked.

He opened his hand and there was a handful of sterling silver flatware. One of our neighbor's boys just went into their mama's silver chest and took out whatever they needed [for camping]. And I took [the silver] immediately, and called Betty, their mama. She hadn't missed it, but we all knew the silver was hers, so she took it back.

Another story is; one of the boys who would camp on the island had a bugle, and he'd toot that darned bugle at the most ungodly times. In the middle of the night, with all the windows open in our home, we'd hear that ghastly noise. At least, we knew the boys were alive over there.

~ from interview with Marjorie Fordham Trask

Elizabeth "Zip" Ricker and her daughter, Betty, age two, at Fripp Island camp in 1928.

Fripp Island fish camp on the Fourth of July.

Duncan Fordham at five years old aboard the "Owanee," a private yacht owned by Fredrick W. Scheper.

"You'd camp on one island, but you'd hunt and fish 25 or 33,000 acres.

"It was a big tract. *Goin' down the river,* that's what we called it."

- Henry Chambers

Setting Up Camp

By Lee Stokes

Arrive at campsite at O-Dark Thirty.

2:20 AM   Fish camp buddies arrive, go over reasons they are late and why they were not able to bring items assigned.

3:15 AM   Take inventory of items on hand and make plans for morning trip to Snack & Shack Co-op Grocery.

3:30 AM   Reassign plans for who goes to grocery based on who has not reached limit on credit card.

4:00 AM   Re-do inventory of items based on what has not been restocked at fish camp since last visit.

4:15 AM   Pool all cash money due to credit card limits exceeding items needed at camp.

4:40 AM   Plan duty assignments for cooking, cleaning and draw straws for who removes dead animals from bathroom.

5:00 AM   Check generator, no fuel, siphon gas from truck. Finish puking gas, remove spark plug from truck for generator, start generator.

5:30 AM   Clean up from generator fire, dispose of wet mattresses, sleep on floor.

6:00 AM   Wake up to noise from gravel drive, find note from fish camp buddies, "Staying at Miss Dooley's, having breakfast, come join us."

6:10 AM   Can't start truck, missing spark plug and no fuel, cell phone battery dead.

6:30 AM   Get ride to Miss Dooley's in back of bait truck, no room in cab with dogs.

7:20 AM   Arrive at Miss Dooley's, met by angry waitress and fish camp buddies, pay bill.

7:50 AM   Leave Snack & Shack Co-op Grocery and head back to camp.

8:30 AM   Arrive at camp and meet Game Warden, Fire Chief and Sheriff.

9:50 AM   Finish police report, pay fines.

10:30 AM   Ready for fishing, realize missing battery to boat.

3:45 PM   Met wife at Miss Dooley's with battery, also has keys to boat and cell phone charger, explain how I know waitress.

5:10 PM   Take charged battery from truck for boat, replace battery, jump start truck, no gas, siphon gas from other vehicle, get sick.

7:20 PM   Leave Snack & Shack Co-op Grocery with concoction of Seltzer, Honey-Molasses and Epsom Salts. Grocery owner says Miss Dooley's home remedy never fails.

9:00 PM   Sleep in truck, fish camp buddies back at Miss Dooley's, note reads; see you in morning.

5:00 AM   Remove charged battery from boat, put in truck, drive to Miss Dooley's.

6:40 AM   Say good-bye to fishing buddies, have breakfast with Miss Dooley, Grocer, Fire Chief, Game Warden and Sheriff.

7:30 AM   Have new fish camp buddies and fish camp - Miss Dooley's.

A fish camp on Skull Inlet in 1917.

"There were camps all over those islands, and they were all close friends, so anyone could use whatever was there.

"All you had to do was go in and clean the grass out that had grown up so you could maneuver.

"Replace what you used of their provisions and you were home free."   - Henry Chambers

Old Camp

Old Island, located just northwest of Fripp Island, SC, was once owned by a man by the name of Herman Blumenthal. Blumenthal was from Charlotte, NC and a very wealthy, generous man, known for his philanthropy. (The North Carolina Blumenthal Performing Arts Center is an example of his community support.) When Blumenthal purchased Old Island in 1960, the island was home to six fish camps. Blumenthal and the camp owners established lease agreements allowing the camps to remain on the island and the camp members to continue hunting there.

In the late 1980's, Blumenthal decided to donate Old Island to the Nature Conservancy. Ownership of the island transferred in 1992, and, along with the transfer, Blumenthal made an agreement with the Nature Conservancy to honor his leases with the six camps. The camps were each signed to a ten-year lease.

For whatever reasons, two years later, in 1994, the Nature Conservancy gave Old Island to the state of South Carolina. In the early 1990's, the state laid claim to the Sea Islands not privately owned, as well as the marshes around the islands up to the mean high water mark. The state honored the Old Island camps' leases until their expiration date in 2002, but elected not to renew them. The camps were abandoned, and a few years later torn down, except for the camp in these photos.

What made this camp different? The state contracted to have Old Island's camps and docks removed, which took big equipment. This camp is still standing on Old Island because its entrance is a narrow, shallow channel of water, and it is too hard, and expensive, to get that big equipment back there. Instead, the state rendered the camp unusable by removing its windows and doors, and any other "conveniences" attached to the camp. Today, the camp may look worse for wear, but it stands with dignity and with its many memories of good times, good food and good friends.[7]

7. Information gathered during interview with person who asked to remain anonymous.

Camp member Sam McGowan at Old Island camp in 1944. McGowan learned to hunt and fish when he was only five or six years old. His experience has passed down through family generations.

Pens like this were used to collect the hunting dogs after a deer drive. It wasn't uncommon for there to be several dog pens located at various positions within the area of the drive.

This camp dates back to 1943.

Sausage Boy

By Gibbes McDowell

Johnson Creek Camp behind Hunting Island was in terrible shape when I bought it in 1995. It had been abandoned for several years. Part of the roof was gone. Rats infested the walls and insulation. It had to be stripped bare and rebuilt. Working weekends to rebuild the camp meant sleeping outside on the ground around the fire until the building was habitable.

Now, as everyone who grew up camping in the Lowcountry knows, you never sleep directly downwind of an open campfire in windy weather. Sparks fly. On a particularly cold trip to the camp there were four of us, three camp members and a friend, who volunteered a weekend's work in return for a little fishing, cold beer, and a steak. Done deal! The night time weather was really cold, about 30 degrees with a wind chill of around 20. We built a large fire and began laying out our sleeping bags. The new guy got the downwind side. We warned him about sparks, telling him, "Let the fire burn down to coals before you go to sleep so you won't have sparks falling on you." But did he listen? He had a cheap summer bag rated to 45 degrees or so. Our wind chill was around 20. He woke up cold and decided to put more wood on the fire. Then he had the bright idea of wrapping his sorry sleeping bag in a sheet of plastic we used to cover lumber.

We woke up the next morning to find that sparks from the fire had shrink wrapped our friend in his sleeping bag. The melted plastic tarp was so tight he couldn't move anything except his face. This was too good to pass up! He looked like a Jimmie Dean Sausage. We rolled him around the yard calling him "sausage boy." The dog threatened to pee on him. He hollered and cussed. This was GREAT. After our friend had sweated himself into a blue funk, we offered to cut him loose if he promised to take it in good fun. You know, that guy never did come back to Johnson Creek Camp.

The "men's tent" on Bay Point in the early 1900's.

"When asked if he would like a beer, Ned said. 'Yeah, but let me finish my coffee first.'"

- Vinnie Rhodes,
*taken from
a fish camp journal*

General Truths About Fish Camps

By Lee Stokes

Given the enormous number of fish camps located in the Lowcountry very few maxims have universal application. There are those, however, that you may wish to commit to memory.

- The quality of the camp is in direct proportion to the quality of the motels in the immediate vicinity.

- Quality fish camps do not have … rows of painted rocks in the drive, large signs pointing to the nearest exit, portable toilets or fish processing plants on the premises.

- Any canned food left in the cupboards which has the dimensions of a softball should be considered hazardous.

- If the camp has an outhouse register you may consider another camp.

- Fish Camps – An extended form of vacation by sleeping in the woods in which people carry double the amount of gear they need for half the time they intend to stay.

"We were all out on the front porch one crisp fall morning drinking coffee.

"The marsh turns a gold color then. It seems like you can see forever in the distance. Someone says, 'I wonder what the rich people are doing.'"

- Lew Gibson

"After four days at Spit Island, we fell into a rhythm, an ebb and flow and into the natural mystic."

- John Trask, *taken from a fish camp journal*

This yacht is believed to be the "Arbutus," owned by Claude Eugene McLeod. The family went down the river many times in this yacht, as well as the "Zorayda," also owned by C. E. McLeod.

The "Zorayda" had beautiful lines from bow to stern. The wicker furniture on the back deck suggests she was made for comfortable cruising.

Flatware

Marjorie McLeod Fordham, daughter of C. E. McLeod, once shared with her daughter, Marjorie Fordham Trask, her memory of one of the family cruises on either the "Zorayda" or the "Arbutus." She was five years old and she recalled dropping the family's silver flatware out the porthole one piece at a time. Somewhere in the Sea Islands may be a setting for eight!

 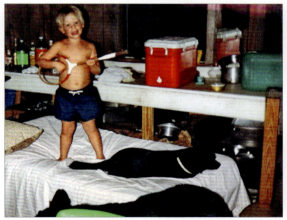 

Top: The 21st century "boys of summer" at a fish camp.

Bottom: A winter trip to camp to "check things out, honey." Odd how many buddies showed up to help.

Top: A sacred fish camp ritual: Men-only day of artery-clogging food and beer.

Bottom: Patrick Mitchell, age five, playing air guitar at the camp. He must be pretty good because his dog hasn't left yet.

Top: Miller Gallant, age four, with two friends: Bubba the dog and a big ol' crawfish.

Bottom: Bay Point fish camp, March 1978. L to R: Red Mitchell, Bacot Alston, Mac McLeod.

Top: Departing from the old loggers' camp on Edding Island after a successful duck hunt, 1955. The bateaus are loaded up with camping gear and game. (Photo taken by Charles T. Paysinger)

Bottom: St. Phillips Island fish camp in 1964.

Top: The loggers' camp on Edding Island was used for one year as trees were logged off the island, after which the camp was abandoned and became a fish camp used on a first-come basis. This day's hunt in 1955 brought in mallard ducks and a deer. (Photo taken by Charles T. Paysinger)

Bottom: A winter visit to their fish camp "Huff-N-Puff."
L to R: Margot H. Rowland, Sandy Peabody, Clark Peabody, Margaret R. VerStraten, and Kate R. Peabody. According to Dr. Larry Rowland, his wife, Margot, named the camp after asking him, "What do you guys do when you go out there? Oh, I know, you huff and puff." (Photo taken by Brian VerStraten)

Top: September 7, 1925, Marjorie McLeod Fordham and her very good friend Virginia Burckmyer posed for the camera off the back end of a bateau.

Bottom: L to R: Hardee McLeod, Fred Ricker, Edith Chandler and a canine companion on the boardwalk at Fripp Island camp in August 1926.

Excerpt from English III Essay

by Nancy Ricker [Rhett]
[written in approximately 1956]

"The island is called Pritchard's; it's just east of Beaufort on the ocean, and that is where we camp each summer: my father and several of his friends, about fifteen young people of assorted ages, Steven the cook, and a lame Labrador retriever named George.

To get to the island we must weave our way through twenty miles of creeks and shallows by boat. One year we went in a shrimp boat. It's wonderful for carrying the big loads of bedding and the blocks of ice, but the results are not worth it: we ran aground in Skull's Inlet and had to swim for shore. Then we had to wait for a higher tide to unload the boat. After the cargo was placed on the beach, we had to walk for two miles to our campsite, and each person was required to make three trips with the loads.

We camp in tents, carry our water unless we're sure of rain, catch our food, and have a lot of fun. We drag a seine, go clamming, fishing and crabbing, sometimes hunting.

There is a little red Jeep that was carried down on a shrimp boat once. If we bring the gas and are not destructive to the Jeep, we can use it, which we do to the fullest extent. To start it, a battery must be attached to something under the hood while someone struggles to keep the Jeep at a standstill. Also, there are not any lights on the front or on the back or anywhere. This can be trying, especially at night, but we have a huge spotlight which can be wired to the battery. However, someone must sit on the hood, which can become quite warm and blistering, and hold the light …."

Erosion

High tide has undermined the legs of this camp. Notice the reinforcements that have been added to the camp's supports to buy time.

Nature's only promise is that she will change things. As she created the Sea Islands via hurricanes and storm surges carving ridges in the creeks and rivers, nature will surely one day take them away in similar fashion. A hurricane, for example, could change the contours of the islands once again, pushing ground and sand from one spot to the next, and putting water over what is now dry ground. Oyster beds could become high ground. Beaches could be moved downstream. Steady natural erosion has its effect even without large storms.

Likewise, fish camps are subject to nature's ways. A lightning strike or a violent storm could take out a camp overnight. Some camps were not built to last forever, because it is a given that the next hurricane will likely wash it away. Fire is also a viable threat. Without a bridge for the fire trucks, a 911 call from a Sea Island isn't going to save a camp struck by lightning. This may seem like a sad fact of life, but reflect on why the fish camp was built there to begin with. Goin' down the river, getting away from it all, includes paying the price that nature demands for her product.

The waters in this inlet have greatly changed course since the camp was built, and what was once solid ground has eroded away. A retaining wall appears to be losing the battle.

The Camps

Some fish camps are spartan, some nearly offer all the conveniences of home, and some are downright "comfortably-seedy." Some camps are seventy-plus years old, and some have been built in the last few years. While age does not necessarily beget beauty, it does seem to add to the authentic vibe you get when you step onto the dock and get your first glimpse of the camp.

And then there is character. The more the better. Camp is about fun. It's mandatory that you leave your stress, and your cell phone, at home. (Okay, one person can bring a phone in case of emergencies.) Feel free to pop a beer and drop a line in the water off the dock, or take a hammer to the loose boards on the porch. Then fire up the grill to cook up the mess of fish caught today. Later, shoot some skeet or tell some wild, half-truth stories around a fire.

Now you've got it … being at fish camp is about living.

"I saw the most amazing shooting star
flaring low across the sky and burning east to west.
Suddenly it shattered into four pieces and disappeared.
No one will believe it!"

- John Trask, *taken from a fish camp journal*

Rattlers Safer Than Football

In the mid-30's, my brother and I would get out of high school on a Friday afternoon, jump in a bateau with a three horsepower outboard and a close friend for a weekend-long camping trip. My mother wouldn't see us again until Sunday afternoon. She would not know which one of those barrier islands [we were on]. She wouldn't know where we went with our hunting dog. But that was okay with her 'cause we'd been enough times with our father. He taught us well. But play football at high school – no way. No way! We could go down there amongst all those rattlesnakes, and there were so many rattlesnakes on some of those islands. In spite of all those hazards and the ride over there carrying weapons, [even] when we were 11 and 12 years old, that was fine with my mother, but play football … you can get hurt doing that. ~ *from interview with anonymous camp owner*

Digging up sea turtle nests and collecting the eggs for cooking or, in this case, eating raw, was common place on the Sea Islands before the turtle became a protected species.

"Approach the dock at the speed you want to hit it."

- Marvin H. Dukes Jr., *taken from a fish camp journal*

Cotton Island Greyhound Bus Camp

Around **1959 or 1960,** Henry C. Chambers and some friends tent camped on Cotton Island to hunt and fish. The group tent camped for five or six years, before bringing over a stripped down Greyhound bus to use as their fish camp. The bus was positioned along the side of the river. A well was drilled, and a pressure pump and tanks were added so the men would have running water. It was the only camp on the island. "We hunted and fished out there for maybe ten years," said Mr. Chambers.

The fish camp was allowed on the island via a handshake agreement with the property owner, which was the way most camps worked at that time, according to Mr. Chambers. It was understood that the fish camp could stay there until such time that the property was sold. When Cotton Island was sold around 1970, the group removed the bus without question. They later set up a new camp, "a much more rustic one this time," on another island half a mile down the river.

The Outhouse Prank

By Gibbes McDowell

Jack Woods, Ned Brown, Junie Levin, and Miles Murdaugh were lifelong fishing buddies and members of "The Capers Island Cats." They had a fish camp on Capers Island back in the 1960's where they spent every available weekend. Each trip to the camp rewarded them with a unique memory, many of which involved pulling a prank on the unsuspecting; especially a new guy in camp. One such occasion involved a friend who was terrified of snakes. Such a phobia was fertile ground for the devious minds of this group. As the evening around the campfire wore on, stories of the large rattlesnakes known to live on barrier islands made the new guy increasingly nervous. The "Cats" made sure this was on his mind when they turned in for the night.

A large "down the river" breakfast of eggs, grits, bacon, biscuits, and lots of strong coffee inevitably led to a trip to the outhouse for the new guy. He was warned to watch out for rattlesnakes. Everybody knows rattlesnakes like to hide around old buildings like outhouses, they reminded him. The trap was laid. As the guest attended to his business, Ned and Junie started talking about a large snake they killed around camp just last weekend. Meanwhile, Jack had sneaked around to the back of the outhouse with an old coat hanger he had made into a long wire with a hook at the end. The new guy was hollering to Ned and Junie to quit the snake talk, when Jack fished his wire hook through a crack in the outhouse wall, found his target with a quick yank and yelled, SNAKE!!!! New guy burst through the outhouse door knocking it flat to the ground, his pants around his knees, crying, "It bit me. A rattlesnake bit me in my ass." Ned and Junie fell off the porch in hysterics. Jack rolled breathless on the ground gasping for air. It took the rest of the weekend for new guy to find the humor in this affair. But, as these stories tend to do, they become interwoven in the fabric of camp lore and lifetime memories that are part of the "down the river" mystique.

"Camp camaraderie by its nature requires everyone to pitch in to make the camp work. Chopping firewood, fixing a leaky roof, building a dock, cooking, etc. brings everyone to the same level. A big job title back *on the hill* (aka the boat landing) doesn't mean much if you don't know which end of a shovel does the work."

- Gibbes McDowell

A Day's Catch - Given the size of the fish on the far left, one of these men may not be too proud of his day's catch.

"Capers Island Cats" in the 1960's. L to R: Charlie Mitchell, Red Mitchell, Cecil Mitchell (center), father of Red and Mac, Mac Mitchell, Bo Mitchell and his father Bud Mitchell.

August 1918, marooning at a fish camp on Skull Inlet.

Fripp Island fish camp, 1920's.

Bay Point fish camp, March 1978.

Special Thanks

When I seriously began to create this book, it didn't take too long before I realized that I had little idea of what I was getting into. I liken the experience to the first time I stepped from Gibbes McDowell's boat into pluff mud. The bottom looked solid from where I stood in the boat, but when I put my boots into the water, and the soft, silky mud began to suck me in, I had one of those terrifying nano-seconds when you realize what you thought was real was only an illusion. I was not on solid ground. Instinct, or something of the sort, told me immediately to make a choice. Freeze in my tracks and let the mud defeat me, or keep moving, risking the loss of my boots, a face-first fall into the water, and, worst of all, the loss of my pride and my camera. I made the choice to keep moving, just as I have with this book.

I have not done it alone. Every step along the way, I have had help from people who have generously given me the benefit of their experience, knowledge and time. There are many.

Gibbes McDowell was my guide to the Sea Islands' fish camps, and the only person on earth who can attest to my near face plant into the pluff mud. He offered up many stories about his experiences *goin' down the river,* and he has been a constant supporter of the goal of this book to share the tradition and lifestyle that fish camps are all about. I was truly honored, and grateful, when I asked Gibbes if he would write the Forward for the book, and his response was "Hell, yes!" It only seems appropriate that since Gibbes was involved toward the beginning that he also take part in the final steps of this project.

Thanks go to every person who has encouraged me, shared his or her stories with me, and entrusted me to communicate, both visually and verbally, the life experiences, the history and the traditions that surround the fish camps. My special thanks go to Henry C. Chambers, Robert Gallant, Pierre McGowan, Lew Gibson, Nancy Rhett, Dr. Lawrence Rowland, Alex Spencer, Lee Stokes, John Trask, Marjorie Fordham Trask, the owners of the camps who gave me permission to photograph their camps, and so many others who contributed in countless ways. Deep gratitude for the older photos, which I believe enrich the book, is given to Pierre McGowan, Marge Mitchell, Nancy Rhett, Margot Rowland, and Marjorie Fordham Trask. And my appreciation goes out to Roger Comes for his tenacious proofing skills.

    Lastly, but of course not the least, I must thank my husband, Bud Garrity. Bud has been my mentor, business partner, friend, editor, admirer and, many times, my inspiration for twenty-five years. Bud, I know you've got my back, and that has given me the courage to jump out of the boat and forge forward with this book. Sink or swim, you don't know unless you try, right? Thank you for telling me to "do it."